ACKNOWLEDGEMENTS:

First and foremost, I would like to thank Oprah Winfrey for bringing to light a difficult subject matter that most people struggle to speak about: Child sexual abuse awareness. Oprah, your voice and courage empowered me to speak up and to make positive change. I no longer live in silence and shame and Ms. Winfrey you are to be credited for that.

I would like to thank my fellow advocates for all of your support. Please continue to fight the good fight and never give up!

Mr. John Robert Luciano, my friend and Lead Editor of this book. Thank you for your support and expertise.

Lastly, and far from least, to my family, you are my beginning, middle, and end. The World is a special place because of you. MRM, you are my light and the air that I breathe.

www.nosecretsbetweenus.com

www.rosemorrisroe.com

About the Author and Illustrator

Author: ROSE MORRISROE, MAT- Rosey is the founder of Soldiers Against Child Abuse, a 501C3 national non-profit organization whose focus is to make a positive impact on the lives of all children and parents. She has written child safety curriculum currently being considered by schools across the country. When Rosey isn't writing or teaching, she is a public speaker who has been interviewed for newspapers and on television at many key events for child safety. She holds a Masters in Education and is an educator in an inner city school district. Rosey has dedicated her life to her calling...raising awareness, education, and intervention in order to protect the most innocent citizens....our children.

Illustrator: Matthew Fox has been doing illustration for over two decades in both publishing and entertainment.

No Secrets Between Us

Author
Rose Morrisroe, MAT

Illustrations by
Matthew Fox

Notes

Sammie has a story to tell.

One day Sammie visited a friend's house.

Sammie played a lot of fun games and enjoyed pool time with everyone.

Finally, all the kids became exhausted from hours of playing in the pool.

A parent named Mr. James said to Sammie,
"It is time to change out of your wet bathing suit
and put on dry clothes."

" I can help you change into dry clothes, Sammie. Come with me into my room. It will be fun!"

" I have a fun game, but it's a secret."
He touches Sammie's private parts and said,
"You can't tell anyone! It's a secret between us."

Sammie is confused and scared. Sammie's parents have told her that the body parts covered by a bathing suit are private. They are personal and not to be touched.

After the party, a friend noticed Sammie looked sad. She asked her, "What is wrong?" So, Sammie told her the secret.

Sammie's friend said, "My Mommy and Daddy tell me there are no secrets between us. You should tell your parents what happened."

Sammie's eyes opened wide as she
remembered Mr. James said,
"It's a secret between us."

When Sammie got home, she thought about it and decided to tell. "Mommy and Daddy, I have to tell you something." Sammie told them the secret.

Sammie's parents were happy and proud that Sammie was brave enough and told them about the secret. They told Sammie it's never the child's fault. But they were very upset with Mr. James.

" Sammie, there should never be any secrets between parents and their children. Mr. James was wrong to touch your private parts - no adult or anyone should ever do that. You should never keep such a secret to yourself. Always tell us or a trusted adult."

Sammie learned that kids in need of help should go to a teacher, family member, friends or a trusted adult. Sammie is very happy now and feels empowered. Sammie knows there are No Secrets Between Us.

Lesson Plan For Educators and Parents, Types of Touches, (K-3rd)
Standard: CCSS: 2.1.2.D.2

Essential Question: What is a safe and unsafe touch? How are they different and should an Unsafe touch be kept a secret?

Objective: To review child sexual abuse. Students/child will learn the kinds of touches: Safe and UNsafe. Students will learn that certain body parts are private.

Materials:

No Secrets Between Us by Rose Morrisroe
Worksheet "There are Different Kinds of Touches"
Drawing paper

Procedure:
Let's play a game about our bodies – "Simon Says"
Simon Says touch your arm, Simon Says touch your leg, Simon Says touch your head, Simon Says touch your chin. Simon says touch your nose. These touches are SAFE. Simon should *never* say to touch the parts of your body that are covered by a bathing suit. No one should ever touch your private parts (Parts covered by a bathing suit.)
We're going to read a book about our body and safe and unsafe touches. The book is titled "No Secrets Between Us." What do you think this book will be about?

As book is read and/or after book is read, suggested questions:

1. What are the parts of your body that are private?
2. Why did Sammie get scared?
3. What are necessary touches? (Hugging, doctor exam, holding a peers hand)
4. What are Safe and Unsafe touches?
5. If someone touches your private parts, should it be a secret?
6. What should you say if someone were to Unsafe touch you?
7. Who can you tell if you are touched on your private parts?
8. If the child did not tell the parents, who else could she/he tell?
9. If you were Sammie would you have told your friend about the Unsafe touching?
10. How did Sammie feel at the end of the book?

Assessment: Students will be able to correctly identify Safe and Unsafe Touches.

Project/Reinforcing the Lesson: Students will work on "There are different kinds of touches" worksheet. When finished, students will write a letter to someone they trust about safe touches and how being aware of types of touches is empowering.

Lesson Plan For Educators and Parents, Types of Touches, (K-3rd)
Standard: CCSS: 2.1.2.D.2

Essential Question: When should you never keep a secret? Should you tell someone if you are touched on your private parts?

Objective: To review child sexual abuse. Students/child will learn how to not keep a secret if someone touched their private parts. Students will learn that certain body parts are private.

Materials:

No Secrets Between Us by Rose Morrisroe
Worksheet "There are Different Kinds of Touches"
Writing paper
Super Hero Award cut out

Procedure:

Let's play a game about our bodies – "Simon Says"
Simon Says touch your arm, Simon Says touch your leg, Simon Says touch your head, Simon Says touch your chin. Simon says touch your nose. These touches are okay. Simon should ***never*** say to touch the parts of your body that are covered by a bathing suit. No one should ever touch your private parts (Parts covered by a bathing suit.)
We're going to read a book about our body and keeping secrets. The book is titled "No Secrets Between Us." What do you think this book will be about?

As book is read and/or after book is read, suggested questions:

1. What are the parts of your body that are private? (Parts covered by a bathing suit)
2. What made Sammie become afraid?
3. What are necessary touches? (Hugging, doctor exam, holding a peers hand, medical care)
4. If someone touched your private parts, should it be a secret?
5. What should you say if someone were to touch your private parts?
6. Who can you tell if you are touched on your private parts?
7. If the child did not tell the parents the secret, who else could she/he tell?
8. If you were Sammie would you have told your friend about the Secret?
9. How did Sammie feel at the end of the book?

Assessment: Students will be able to correctly identify their private parts and understand when it's not appropriate to keep secrets.

Project/Reinforcing the Lesson: Students will work on "There are different kinds of touches" worksheet. When finished, students will write a letter to a person they would trust to tell if they had a secret. Lastly, students will cut out the "Super Hero" clip art and wear it proudly!!! ☺

Directions: Now that you've read, "No Secrets Between Us," and you know how to protect yourself, you've earned a Super Hero Award! Cut out the Super Hero award, and tape it to your shirt. Wear it with pride, Super Hero!

VOCABULARY

Brave: A person/child who shows courage.

Empower: Taking charge of your own life and body.

Private Parts: Body parts covered by a bathing suit; personal.

Safe: Free from harm or risk.

Secret: Kept hidden from people; not telling anyone.

Trusted Adult: A person you trust and feel safe with.

CCSS.ELA-Literacy.L.1.4 Determine or clarify the meaning of unknown and multiple-meaning words and phrases based on *grade 1 reading and content*, choosing flexibly from an array of strategies.
CCSS.ELA-Literacy.L.1.4a Use sentence-level context as a clue to the meaning of a word or phrase.
CCSS.ELA-Literacy.L.1.4b Use frequently occurring affixes as a clue to the meaning of a word.
CCSS.ELA-Literacy.L.2.4 Determine or clarify the meaning of unknown and multiple-meaning words and phrases based on grade 2 reading and content, choosing flexibly from an array of strategies.
CCSS.ELA-Literacy.L.2.4a Use sentence-level context as a clue to the meaning of a word or phrase.
CCSS.ELA-Literacy.L.3.4 Determine or clarify the meaning of unknown and multiple-meaning word and phrases based on grade 3 reading and content, choosing flexibly from a range of strategies.
CCSS.ELA-Literacy.L.3.4a Use sentence-level context as a clue to the meaning of a word or phrase.

SIGHT WORDS: K-3RD Grade

After	Always	But	Everyone
Finally	Friend	House	Look
Now	One	Said	That
The	Them	There	Very
With	You		

CCSS: RF.K.3 (a-g), RF.1.3(a-g), RF.2.3(a-g), RF.3.3(a-g)

MODEL CURRICULUM STANDARDS RELATED TO THIS BOOK: K-3rd Grade

Vocabulary Acquisition and Use

1.RIT.4: Ask and answer questions to help determine or clarify the meaning of words and phrases in a text.
L.K.1, L.1.1, L.2.1, L.3.1: Demonstrate command of the conventions of standard English grammar and usage when writing or speaking.
L.K.4, L.1.4, L.2.4, L.3.4: Determine or clarify the meaning of unknown and multiple-meaning words and phrases based on grade reading and content, choosing flexibly from an array of strategies.

Sight Words/Decoding Words/Identify and Read Grade Level HF Words

RF.K.3 (a-g), RF.1.3(a-g), RF.2.3(a-g), RF.3.3(a-g)

Literacy; Conventions of Standard English

L.K.2, L.1.2, L.2.2, L.3.2: Demonstrate command of the conventions of Standard English capitalization, punctuation, and spelling when writing.
L.K.1a, L.1.1a, L.2.1a, L.3.1a: Print all upper- and lowercase letters.
L.K.2b, L.1.2b, L.2.2b, L.3.2b: Use end punctuation for sentences.

Writing Standard

W.K.3, W.1.3, W.2.3, W.3.3: Write narratives in which they recount two or more appropriately sequenced events, include some details regarding what happened, use temporal words to signal event order, and provide some sense of closure.
W.3.3.a: Establish a situation and introduce a narrator and/or characters within a piece of writing. i.e. Students could make a connection between Sammie in the book and what they should do in that situation.
W.K.6, W.1.6, W.2.6, W.3.6: With guidance and support from adults, use a variety of productions to produce and publish writing (a letter) including in collaboration with peers.

Reading; Key Ideas and Details

RL.K.1, RL.1.1, RL.2.1, RL.3.1: Ask and answer questions about key details in a text.
RL.K.2, RL.1.2, RL.2.2, RL.3.2 : Retell stories, including key details, and demonstrate understanding of their central message or lesson.
RL.K.3, RL.1.3, RL.2.3, RL.3.3: Describe characters, settings, and major events in a story, using key details.

Endorsements

"Rose Morrisroe: one of the top educational instructors for the state of New Jersey and founder for one of the leading non-profits on child abuse prevention - *Soldiers Against Child Abuse*. She encompasses vision, awareness, passion and accomplishment to the world she touches....She saves the world around her and embraces the hurt with healing, guidance and compassion."

~Michael Reagan

"The Governor is grateful for your interest in offering your book, *No Secrets Between Us*, and curriculum for use in schools throughout the State and has shared the information you sent with the appropriate staff in the Department of Education. The Governor is grateful for your support and joins me in offering you best wishes."

~Governor Christie's Office via Staffer

"Rose Morrisroe is a revered educator and survivor of child sexual abuse. She advocates for empowering children and families. Her wonderful book, *No Secrets Between Us,* is an important tool to the prevention of child abuse. *No Secrets Between Us* teaches children to empower themselves when they feel unsafe. CSA is an uncomfortable topic which needs to be discussed and this book is an effective means to do that."

~Kathleen Shelley, LSW - School Social Worker

"As a Licensed Certified Social Worker I plan on using the book, *No Secrets Between Us*, at home as well as with my clients at work. You have provided me with an educational tool that will be heard by many children and recommended to every parent I know."

~Jacqueline Russak, LCSW- School Social Worker

"This is a must book for all parents, guardians and educators. Rose Morrisroe not only demonstrates the need for children to be proactive but she prepares parents in how to empower the family. I wish this book was available when my kids were younger. This book is empowering for all children."

~Michael John Sullivan -- Award winning author and creator of The SockKids Children's series

"*No Secrets Between Us* is a great introduction for parents and children to begin a dialogue about safe and unsafe touches. It is child friendly and well written which encourages honest and open dialogue. I recommend Mrs. Morrisroe's book for all children."

~Wanda Merchant, LPC - Licensed Professional Counselor
School Counselor, Anti-Bullying Specialist

"*No Secrets Between Us* by Rose Morrisroe is a great tool for parents and educators in assisting with this challenging topic. Mrs. Morrisroe is clearly dedicated to her cause and through her book has created a child friendly way to deliver a powerful message. This book is designed to empower children and families."

~Nicole C. Syperski, M.A.
School Counselor, Intervention & Referral Services

Made in the USA
Lexington, KY
16 June 2015